# ITATICS

The [f]aCT
of the mATTER
is that mE and
'U' are each II
with n-ATURA

sENSEfully
& bODYfully
oTHERiNG
n-ATURA

**n-ATURA**
the not 'U' & mE
biT and 'U' & mE
the miNEfully
thiNEfully
oTHER'd biTs

and when
'U' & mE the not
not oTHER'd
biTs bODYfully
separate each
oTHER
out from
n-ATURA
wE then
become
III 'U' mE
and iT

**Know the**
**:( fEELiNG :)**

iT:the many
sided not
yoU and
mE bit of
n-ATURA

and when
'U' and I the not
not oTHER'd biTs
confront then the
d-eMPTY bACK
& beYOND of the
'mE yoU and iT'
in-bETWEEN
'U" and I can
settle then
for IV

becoming in
the process
oNE with
n-ATURA
thro' the
d-EMPTY
IVth set of
iT's bACK
& beyond

n-ATURA
that 4D
sPACETiME
conTiNUUM
that miNEfuLL
tHiNEfuLL
in-bETWEEN
conTiNUUM

that collapses
bODYfully in
to a pHYSiCAL
sPACED oUT 3D'd
conTiNUUM

alongside a
tiMED oUT
3D'ing mU
mENTAL
conTiNUUM

**configured
in terms of
|266|-tUPLED
[m]UmENTAL
LOCATiONs**

discrete
LOCATiONs
topping those
bODiLY oNEs of
pHYSiCAL sPACE

constantly
conjoined
mENTAL &
pHYSiCAL
LOCATiONs

in-bETWEEN
LOCATiONs
identified
each
through
specific
mU mode'd
LOCUTiONs

sENSE
fuLL sPEAKing
bODYs wE aLL
fACELess bODYs
inFANTiLY located
somewhere within
mUmENTAL sPACE

sPACiALLY placed
mU sENSiCAL rAG
bAGs of infANTiLE
(m)A and {d}A
fEELiNGs and
tHOUGHTs

**sPACED oUT
LOCATiONs both
mENTAL and
pHYSiCAL**

sPACED oUT mE
& 'U' LOCATiONs
unmATCHed
& mATCHing
miNORed &
miNORing

mU mENTAL
LOCATiONs bODiLY
located within
LiNGuisticaLLY
constructed
mUNiTARY
gROUPings

[w]E singular
mUNiTARY
gROUPings both
miNOR & mAJOR

gROUPed
gROUPings of
fAMiLY tRiBE
cLAN and sTATE
nATiON sTATE

strUCTured each by
the mis-matched
and matching
free-play of
miNOR and
mAJOR sub
setted set
gROUP
ings

fiVE
approvingly
bARBAROUS
d-aCT I
mAJORs

fiVE
d-aCT I
potentially
sAVAGE
d-aCT II
miNORs

# [m]U
## mAJOR
### gROUPings

# d-aRiSTOCRATiC
# miN-miNORing
# gROUPings

miLiTARiSTiC
miN-miNORing
oTHERs

# d-oUT oF iT
## miN-miNORing
### gROUPings

# tHEOCRATiC
# miN-miNORing
# oTHERs

# cRiTiCoCRATiC
# miN-miNORing
# gROUPings

exploitative
gROUPings

grounded
in mutually
mirrored
d-eYEfuLLs
of mUsome
d-UPLiCiTY

endLessly
appropriating
tHiNGs tHERE
and tHEIR's

[m]U
miNOR
gROUPings

**approvingly**
**miN-miNORed**

disapprovingly so by
d-aRiSTOCRATiC
gROUPings

domineeringly so by
miLiTARiSTiC
oTHERs

**d-littlingly so by
mediTATiVE oUT
gROUPings**

unfavoringly so by
tHEOCRATiC
oTHERs

**b-ittlingly so by
cRiTiCoCRATiC
gROUPings**

# exploited
## gROUPings

exploited
gROUPings
grounded aLL
in mutually
mirrored
d-eYE
fuLLs of
mUsome
d-eMPATHY

overseen and
structured by
(m)AFiA and {d}AFiA
reactionary [04']
miN-mAJORs

[m]U miNORs
and mAJORs
bound by some
conquering
or chosen
(m)A or {d}A
mATRiARCH or
pATRiARCH

[m]U exhibits
each of oNE
of the [m]U
meNTALs

gROUP
ings grouped
historically by
some commUnally
sponsered bACK
of beYOND
gREATer
bEiNG or
bEiNGs

c-ULTURA the
aRTiFACTUAL
mU mENTaL
cLuTTeR of the
in-beTWEENs of
mis-matched
gROUPings

wORDed
gROUPings
oRAL or tEXT
bound gROUPings
that separate out
gLOBE-ALLY

into fiVE
mis-matched
c-ULTURALs

**c-ULTURALs
grounded in the
primal tHOUGHTs
of hAViNG and
bEiNG**

sPACED oUT
wESTERN
c-ULTURALs
of hAViNG
before
bEiNG

pLATONiC
hAViNGs
of iDEAs
idEAL

cOPies of
'VoGUE'
and the
appealing
'CHRiSTiAN
ReviEW'
bEiNG the
oUTcome

eASTERN
tiMED oUT
c-ULTURALs
of bEiNG
before
hAViNG

dreamt
up aTMANic
seXed oUT
vEDiC fORMs
the kARMic out
pourings of
bRAHMANiC
dEEP sLEEP

mODERN day
'bOLLYWOOD'
hAViNGs

hAViNG
the same
bRAHMANiC
seXed oUT
effects

exiling
spaced out
miDDLE eASTERN
c-ULTURALs of
bEiNG after
hAViNG
been un
fAVORed
LiTTLe
'siNNERs'
rEALLY!?

tORAHNiCAL
biBLiCAL
kORANiCAL
post havings
tHEOLOGiCAL
post havings
of LaW bound
promises
for any
and aLL
siNNing
'siNNERs'

the GAZA
& wEST bANK
bound modern
day post exiled
[i]GROUPing bEiNG
todAY's sAVAGE
unfaVOURing
d-aCT II
oUTcome

tiMELeSSLY
d-oUT of
iT sOUTH
eASTERN
c-ULTURALs
of neither
hAViNG
nOR
bEiNG

oNCE the
noT noT hAViNG
and noT noT bEiNG
d-LUDED oNEs
aNCiENT and
mODERN

dropping
then & now
thoughts
of bODY and
miND whilst
grasping the
eMPTYness of
d-eMPTYness
within their
fULLsome
bUDDA like
siTTings

wALLed
in and oUT
fAR eASTERN
c-ULTURALs of
re-active after
hAViNGs of
not bEiNG

cONFUCiAN
aNALECTiCAL
hAViNGs of
avoiding
not bEiNG
alongside
the nAME
Less d-aCT
III wAYs of
LAO TZU

modern
day pARTY
oFFiCiAL com
forming re
formings the
oUTcome

c-ULTURA the
cLuTTeRed
toPPiNG of
n-aTURA in
beTWEEN
n-aTURA in
between the
d-eMPTYness
of iT's baCK
& beYOND

n-ATURA the
bit numbered
in-beTWEEN
awash with
nUMBERs
that refer to
nOTHING but
themselves each
a simple eCHO
of it's sELF no
different from
any of the
sENSiBLEs

they the
referents of
aLL else

matched
sETTiNGs
of the in
beTWEEN
that sETs
out

fiVe
timed
out heAPs
of sENSiBLEs
iMAGE-fuLLY
bundled and
bagged by
the sPACED
out fORMs of
the iMAGiNARY

the feeling bound
iMAGiNARY backing
both the sENSORY
& the sYMBOLiC

the sounded
out & signifying
sYMBOLiC full of
siGNs and sYMBOLs
that unlike nUMBERs
refer to any & every
identifiable tHiNG

bit-numbered and
numbering siGNs &
sYMBOLs of sENSORY
eVENTs bundled and
bundled by the
fiGURATiVE
fORMs of the
iMAGiNARY

**cOMMON
SENSiCAL
bODYs the
result**

alongside biTs
tHEORETiCAL

name tagged
and numbered
tHEORETiCALs
sTANDiNG under
aLL such bODYS
in-beTWEEN

sENSED and
thOUGHT-oUT
in-beTWEEN
aPPLEs sTARs
and pLANETs

tEORETically
grabbed and
bagged by that
tELESCOPED
Lot in terms of
Spaced & Timed
out mass binding
forces summed up in
Newton's working
formula F=mA and
Einstein's lightsome
energizing $E=mC^2$

sensed and
thOUGHT-out
in-beTWEEN
interference
patterns double
split interference
patterns

tEORETically
grabbed and bagged
by that cOLLiDER probing
Lot in terms of collapsing
force fields of biT point
instants of Quantum
wave particles
located in and
beyond the
backside
edges of
aLL bODYs
in-beTWEEN

completely
captured by
Schrodinger's
Wave equation
$H\Psi=E\Psi$ and
Heisenberg's
equivalent
mATRiCEs

sensed and
thOUGHT-out in
beTWEEN ceLLs nuclei
& organelles

tEORETically
grabbed and bagged by
that probing miCROSCOPED
Lot in terms of chance bound
helically structured genetic
bits of aLL living bODYs
driving and shaping all
known fORMs of
past & present
planetary Life

sensed and
thOUGHT-out
in-beTWEEN
imitative aCTs
miRRORing the
aCTs of oTHER's

tEORETically
grabbed and
bagged by that
sCALPEL probing
Lot in terms
of riZZOLATI's
miRRORing cells
littering the bRAiNS
behind the backside
edges of the bACK
of Chimpanzee's
Dolphin's and
[m]Uman's
sENTiENCE

sensed and
thOUGHT-out
in-beTWEEN
responses to the
[m]U questionings

tEORETically grabbed
and bagged by the
dOCTOR mANNiE
oNE in terms of biT
part miRRORings
of the infantile
entanglements of
some miNEfull
(m)A and {d}A
fAMiLY
aFFAiR

miRRORings
further grabbed
and bagged by that
mATERiALiST Lot in
terms of the transduced
sensory and feeling filled
in-puts central to the
hARDWiRiNG of the in
fANTiLE dendritically
networking nEURONs
underlying the recursive
programming of the
brAiNED-out bit
behind the back
side edge of
the baCK

routine
programming
captured completely
by the [m]U formal
working routines

$(1^{31}2)$  ∃ i ∈ [Ξ]  {1^504'}

**unfavored**     **unfavoring**
**b-atmoi**         **d-jivat'**

{i} = Σ [$(1^{31}2).\{1^504'\}$] = {Ξ}

**d-anatmoi**         **b-jivat'**
**d-littled**         **b-littling**

$(1^31)$    ∃ i ∈ [Ξ]    {1^704'}

modular
(m)ALGO and
{d}ALGORiTHmic
routines shaping all
known forms of past
present & future
adULTESCENT
aFFAiRs

Lastly focus
now on the
cLuTTeRed
d-eMPTYness
of the baCK
the beYOND
& aLL bODYs
in-beTWEEN

The [f]aCT
of the mATTER
remember is
that 'U' & mE
are each II
with n-ATURA

sENSEully
& bODYfully
oTHERing
n-ATURA

n-ATURA
the not 'U' & mE
biT and 'U' & mE
the miNEfully
thiNEfully
oTHER'd biTs

and when
'U' & mE the not
not  oTHER'd
biTs bODYfully
separate each
oTHER
out from
n-ATURA
wE then
become
III 'U' mE
and iT

Remember the
:( fEELiNG :)

iT:the many
sided not
yoU and
mE bit of
n-ATURA

and when
'U' and I  the not
not oTHER'd biTs
confront then the
the d-eMPTY bACK
and beYOND of the
endLessly eNDing
'mE yoU and iT'
in-bETWEEN
'U" and I can
settle then
for IV

becoming one
in the process
with oNEsing
and oNEsied
n-ATURA
thro' the
d-EMPTY
IVth set of
iT's bACK
& beYOND

Printed in Great Britain
by Amazon